...~g

much. . . . .

Sophie xx

because he blows
me raspberries!!

To my grandfather,

_____,

from _____

I love you because . . .

_____

_____

_____

_____

_____ _____, _____
Date

I LOVE MY

Grandfather

BECAUSE . . .

Compiled by
Carolyn J. Booth
and Mindy B. Henderson

RUTLEDGE HILL PRESS ®
Nashville, Tennessee

Published by Rutledge Hill Press®, Inc., 211 Seventh
Avenue North, Nashville, Tennessee 37219. Distributed
in Canada by H. B. Fenn & Company, Ltd., 34 Nixon
Road, Bolton, Ontario L7E 1W2. Distributed in
Australia by Five Mile Press Pty, Ltd., 22 Summit Road,
Noble Park, Victoria 3174. Distributed in New Zealand
by Tandem Press, 2 Rugby Road, Birkenhead,
Auckland 10. Distributed in the United Kingdom by
Verulam Publishing, Ltd., 152a Park Street Lane, Park
Street, St. Albans, Hertfordshire AL2 2AU.

Typography by Compass Communications, Inc.

Design by Bateman Design
Illustrations by Farrar Hood

ISBN: 1-55853-670-1

Printed in the United States of America

1 2 3 4 5 6 7 8 9—02 01 00 99 98

Introduction

The sweetest sound to a grandfather's ears is the voice of his grandchild saying, "I love you." Precious memories are created between a grandfather and his grandchild when they spend time together, and a grandfather's encouragement and unconditional love for his grandchild form a special bond that lasts forever.

In this book, grandchildren of all ages share their reasons for loving their grandfathers. Their words come from the heart—some smile with joy when remembering happy times they spent with their grandfather—others' eyes fill with tears as they recall special memories of a grandfather who is no longer with them.

Your own unique bond with your grandfather is very special. When you think about the reasons why you love your grandfather, write them down. Tell him how much you love him and why he is so precious to you. Give him a kiss and a big hug, and spend some time together making more memories.

One hundred years from now it will not matter what my bank account was, the sort of house I lived in, or the kind of car I drove—but the world may be different because I was important in the life of a child.

—Anonymous

I LOVE MY

Grandfather

BECAUSE . . .

He gives great hugs and sweet
sugar kisses.

⊰⊱⊷⊙⊶⊰⊱

He plays the guitar for me.

He loves me unconditionally.

⊱─◈─○─◈─⊰

He sings silly songs in a silly voice and makes me laugh.

⊱─◈─○─◈─⊰

He answers all my questions. He knows almost everything.

One day my grandson and I
were looking at antiques,
and I was explaining to him the
meaning of the word. He looked
at me and said, "Gramps, are
you an antique?"
I laughed and replied, "I guess I am.
What would you say I'm worth?"
Without missing a beat, he shrugged
and said with a twinkle in his eye,
"You're not for sale."

My grandparents are sweet and easy. She is Sweet and he is Easy—and that's what I call them!

—Lannie Jewell

A little boy is busily and laboriously helping his grandfather wash the car. Soon, one of his grandfather's friends comes upon the two working together. "What's he paying you to help him?" the man asked the young grandson. "Attention!" the boy beamed.

I LOVE MY

Grandfather

BECAUSE . . .

He sneaks treats to me at
dinnertime!

⊳━◆━◦━◈━◅

He gave me his name—
I am a III!

He made me a tree swing.

He helps anyone who
needs help.

He is always honest with me.

Grandchildren learn by experience. I had often told my grandson that my grandfather and I loved to fish together. When he turned five years old, I took him out on my farm to the pond. We sat together, silently, with our hooks in the water. He squirmed a little, as if he were getting bored. Suddenly, his line pulled a bit, and he looked at me and said, "Grandpa, I got a bite!"

He and I reeled the fish in. As I took it off the hook, I knelt to show him his catch. He was grinning ear to ear and then his eyes met mine. There we were grandfather—grandson. A feeling fell over me at that instant, because I knew that suddenly he had experienced it. The love of fishing with his grandfather—a love that would be passed on through to my great-grandchildren.

T̲hrough my grandfather's
eyes I see:
beauty in nature, in people, and
in my grandma.
bravery during the wars that
were fought.
honor in the hard work he has
done to support his family
and in the life he has led.
love for country, for others, for
family, and for God.
hope for me, my children, and
the generations to come.

I love my grandfather
because he always
has time for me.

I LOVE MY

Grandfather

BECAUSE . . .

He pushes me as high as the
sky on my swing.

⊷—❖—⊶

Every Saturday we go
someplace special.

He fixes all my broken toys.

He lets me sleep with him when I'm scared.

He buys tons of my school fund-raising stuff.

AS MY

Grandfather

ALWAYS SAID:

Happiness is success,
not money.

Teach by example, not words.

I don't know who my grandfather was; I'm much more concerned to know who his grandson will be.

—Abraham Lincoln

When I was young, my grandfather and I used to walk around his farm. I tried desperately to step exactly into his footprints. Now, twenty years later, I still try to follow those footsteps. They're just different now—they are integrity, wisdom, and love.

—Lisa Gorman

The righteous man leads a blameless life; blessed are his children after him.

—Proverbs 20:7

I LOVE MY

Grandfather

BECAUSE . . .

I know he loves me.

>–•>–•–O–•<–•<

He picks me up after school and
takes me to get an Icee!

He taught me to use a tire
gauge and to change a tire.

⊳⊢◄►◦◦◄►⊣◅

He puts me on his shoulders at
the Christmas parade.

⊳⊢◄►◦◦◄►⊣◅

He taught me to make model
airplanes.

Grandparents and grandchildren have much to tell each other. One has just come from the spirit world and the other is on his way to the spirit world.

—Tautachcho, Chumash people

I love my grandfather
because
he always has time to
listen—he doesn't get
in a hurry.

WAYS TO HELP YOUR

Grandchildren

REMEMBER YOU . . .

Coach a Little League team.

>─┼─◆>─0─◆─┼─<

Build something together—a
birdhouse, model airplane, or a
tree house.

Volunteer at your
grandchildren's school to read,
tutor, or go on field trips
with them.

Help your grandchildren
start a collection you
can enjoy together.

I LOVE MY

Grandfather

BECAUSE . . .

He taught me to read a map.

>–<>–O–<>–<

He comes for my show-and-tell
at school, and I show him!

He tells me I'm pretty.

▷─┤◆─0─◆┤─◁

When I was young, he took me
on long walks. We would rest
under a tree, and he would say,
"Take time to look around you
and see the beauty."

AS MY

Grandfather

ALWAYS SAID:

You can't love someone you
haven't laughed with.

⊹⊱⟶⊹⟶O⟶⊹⟶⊰⊹

Never drive faster than your
angels can fly.

I'm going to ask something of every one of you. Let me start with my generation, the grandparents out there. You are our living link to the past. Tell your grandchildren the story of the struggles waged, at home and abroad; of sacrifices freely made for freedom's sake. And tell them your own story as well—because every American has a story to tell.

—George Bush

The mental image of a loving grandfather may be a piece of the picture that his grandchildren carry to maturity as a part of their concept of godliness. What an opportunity! What a gift! What a responsibility! Oh, that I can make a difference, an eternal difference, in the lives of children.

—David Booth

I LOVE MY
Grandfather
BECAUSE . . .

We go to ball games. We don't sit; we walk the fence!

>─↦◇─○─◇↤─<

He lives far away, but he calls me every week.

When I don't win, he says,
"The best you can do is
good enough."

⊱━━◦○◦━━⊰

He wrote me encouraging notes
when I was in college.

⊱━━◦○◦━━⊰

He's a doctor, so if I get hurt, he
knows what to do!

> ⊱⊰⊶⊷0⊶⊷⊱⊰ ⊰

M y children call my father King.
One night, as he was watching the
children play on the floor of his den,
he walked over and put his arm
around my shoulders.
"Do you know what, Princess?" he
asked me with tears in his eyes.
"What, Daddy?"

"Any real king would be envious of
the riches that I have right here in
this house right now," he said,
nodding toward my children
and giving me an extra hug.
"We are very blessed,
Daddy," I said.
"With things money can't buy," he
said, and I breathed in that moment
of happiness with my father.

I LOVE MY

Grandfather

BECAUSE . . .

He always says, "You can do it!
Just try!"

⊱━━◆━━○━━◆━━⊰

When my parents divorced, he
helped me understand it was
not my fault.

He showed me how to bait my
hook and catch big fish.

⊳─┼─◈≻─◯─≺◈─┼─⊲

He rides me on his
lawn mower.

⊳─┼─◈≻─◯─≺◈─┼─⊲

He is kind and always
takes up for me.

>⊷⊶◇⊷⊶<

AS MY

Grandfather

ALWAYS SAID:

Don't ever disagree
with a woman.

>⊷⊶◇⊷⊶<

Always pray believing.

I don't know why I call him G-Daddy—maybe it's because he's good, gallant, gracious, gentle, giving, godly, and grand!

My DeDaddy was **de**dicated to his family, **de**lightful to be with, and **de**ar to my heart.

—Becky Henry

I love my grandfather
because
he prays with me.

I LOVE MY

Grandfather

BECAUSE . . .

He gave me my great-grandfather's pocket watch.

⊱—◦—⊰

He helps me with
my homework.

We collect baseball
cards together.

⊱┄•◦•┄⊰

We watch old Western
movies together.

⊱┄•◦•┄⊰

He is very wise.

I f you want good advice,

consult an old man.

—Romanian Proverb

I love my grandfather because he seems always to turn a bad situation into something good.

Your grandchildren are the
most beautiful leaves
on the family tree.

I love my grandfather because he pretends to be the Beast, I pretend to be the Beauty, and we dance.

I was watching the Super Bowl with my ninety-two-year-old grandfather, and our team scored a touchdown. When they showed the instant replay, he thought they scored another one. I was going to tell him, but I figured the game he was watching was better.

—Comedian Steven Wright

Children are a poor
man's wealth.

—Danish Proverb

My grandchildren come to my house once a month for dinner. My wife and I center it on some exciting event in our lives. For instance, one time we had a Civil War dinner. We cooked cornbread and beans. I dressed up in my best 1800s outfit. After dinner, we sat in our den and told stories of my great-grandfather and his family—where they were and what they were doing at the time.

These are memories that my grandchildren will cherish.

AS MY

Grandfather

ALWAYS SAID:

Never turn down anything
that is free.

If it is to be, it is up to me.

Not a tenth of us who are in business are doing as well as we could if we merely followed the principles that were known to our grandfathers.

—William Feather

Give a little love to a child

and you get

a great deal back.

—John Ruskin

All of my grandparents, except one dear, sweet grandpa, were dead before I was ever born. I like to think they were the ones telling me these stories in my dreams, whispering in my ear as I was dozing off, letting me know I was loved.

—Carolyn Kay Armistead

If youth but had the
knowledge and
old age the strength.

—French Proverb

I LOVE MY

Grandfather

BECAUSE . . .

He taught me about
the stock market.

>—•—◦—•—<

He taught me the importance of
a good work ethic.

He is the rock that I cling to in the floods of life—he is the only positive male influence in my life.

>—+—◆►—O—◄◆+—◄

I feel safe when he's around.

>—+—◆►—O—◄◆+—◄

He dances with me.

AS MY

Grandfather

ALWAYS SAID:

Don't be overly impressed with
those in high places. They put
on their pants one leg at a time
just as you do.

Don't ever let your children
believe that you could stop
loving them.

Grandchildren graze, like the deer, on the long gray hair of their grandparents; that is their wisdom.

—Tautachcho, Chumash people

You've got to do your own
growing, no matter how tall
your grandfather was.

—Irish Proverb

I LOVE MY

Grandfather

BECAUSE . . .

He calls me a special nickname.

>—+◊>—○—<◊+—<

He taught me to play golf—and
even made me my first clubs!

He treats me as his friend.

⊳—⊢—◀◊▸—O—◀◊▸—⊣—◁

He treats me like I'm a princess.

⊳—⊢—◀◊▸—O—◀◊▸—⊣—◁

He gave me my first
cowboy hat.

I love my grandfather because he tells me lots of good stories about our family.

Children's children are a crown to the aged.

—Proverbs 17:6

WAYS TO HELP YOUR

Grandchildren

REMEMBER YOU . . .

Put on some music
and dance together.

⊱─┤◆─○─◆├─⊰

Tell your history over and
over in stories.

Have one-on-one time
with each grandchild.

⊱───◉───⊰

Take a walk, or sit together
under a favorite tree and talk.

I LOVE MY

Grandfather

BECAUSE . . .

He brings me treats from his
out-of-town trips.

⊷—◦—⊶

He takes me to the car races.

He is so very funny.

— ⊶ ⊙ ⊷ —

We watch sports together.

— ⊶ ⊙ ⊷ —

He sits outside with me and
we name the stars.

AS MY

Grandfather

ALWAYS SAID:

If it sounds too good to be true,
it probably is.

Hold your head high, no matter
how low you feel.

Our land is everything
to us . . . I will tell you one
of the things we remember
on our land. We remember
that our grandfathers paid
for it—with their lives.

—John Wooden Legs, Cheyenne

In the end it's not the years in your life that count, it's the life in your years.

—Abraham Lincoln

Treat the earth well: it was
not given to you by your
parents, it was loaned to
you by your children. We
do not inherit the Earth
from our ancestors, we
borrow it from our children.

—Ancient Native-American Proverb

I LOVE MY

Grandfather

BECAUSE . . .

He helped coach our Little
League team.

⊱⊰◦⊱⊰

He lets me help feed the
cows on his farm.

He gave me my first Bible
with a very special note in it
from him to me.

⊱━◈━०━◈━⊰

He took me hiking and taught
me how to love the outdoors.

⊱━◈━०━◈━⊰

He dug a grave and helped me
bury my dog. We both cried.

My grandfather once told me that there are two kinds of people: those who work and those who take the credit. He told me to be in the first group; there was less competition there.

—Indira Gandhi

A grandfather was walking
through his yard when he heard his
granddaughter repeating the
alphabet in a tone of voice that
sounded like a prayer. He asked her
what she was doing.

The little girl explained, "I'm
praying, but I can't think of exactly
the right words, so I'm just saying all
the letters. God will put them
together for me, because he knows
what I am thinking.

I love my grandfather
because
he is a great cook!

$\rightarrowtail\!\!-\!\!\leftrightarrow\!\!-\!\!O\!\!-\!\!\leftrightarrow\!\!-\!\!\rightarrowtail$

My grandfather is sacred to me. Sometimes when I close my eyes, I can feel his spirit move through me like the wind. It reminds me that he lives on through me and my children.

AS MY

Grandfather

ALWAYS SAID . . .

Play dead if a bear is
coming.

If you see a good-looking
girl, ask her out.

I LOVE MY

Grandfather

BECAUSE . . .

He takes me to his office and
tells everyone how smart I am.

⊱━━◦━━◦━━◦━━⊰

He treats all my friends to
burgers after our ball games.

He always carries gum to give
to me and my friends.

⊳─┼─◆─0─◆─┼─⊲

He follows the Golden Rule.

⊳─┼─◆─0─◆─┼─⊲

He gives me all his old hats.

A good man leaves an inheritance for his children's children.

—Proverbs 13:22

I love my grandfather
because he loves
my grandmother.

LITTLE EYES UPON YOU

There are little eyes upon you
And they're watching
    night and day.
There are little ears that quickly
Take in every word you say.
There are little hands all eager
To do anything you do;
And a little boy who's dreaming
Of the day he'll be like you.

You're the little fellow's idol,
You're the wisest of the wise.
In his little mind about you
No suspicions ever rise.
He believes in you devoutly,
Holds all you say and do;
He will say and do, in your way
When he's grown up
just like you.

There's a wide-eyed little fellow
Who believes you're
    always right;
And his eyes are always opened,
And he watches day and night.
You are setting an example
Every day in all you do;
For the little boy who's waiting
To grow up to be like you.

—Anonymous